SALT AND LIGHT
POCKET GUIDES

COMING TO GRIPS WITH
HEAVEN

COMING TO GRIPS WITH
HEAVEN

ERWIN W. LUTZER

MOODY PRESS
CHICAGO

© 1990 by
THE MOODY BIBLE INSTITUTE
OF CHICAGO

All Scripture quotations, unless noted otherwise, are from the *New American Standard Bible*, © 1960, 1962, 1963, 1968, 1971, 1972, 1973, 1975, and 1977 by The Lockman Foundation, and are used by permission.

ISBN: 0-8024-3541-6

1 2 3 4 5 6 7 8 Printing/VP/Year 95 94 93 92 91 90

Printed in the United States of America

Coming to Grips with
Heaven

In the Middle East a fable is told of a Baghdad merchant who sent his servant to the marketplace to run an errand. When he had completed his assignment and was about to leave the marketplace, he turned a corner and unexpectedly met Lady Death. The look on her face so frightened him that he left the marketplace and hurried home. He told his master what had happened and requested his fastest horse so that he could get as far from Lady Death as possible— a horse that would take him all the way to Sumera before nightfall.

Later that same afternoon the merchant himself went to the marketplace and met Lady Death. "Why did you startle my servant this morning?" he asked.

"I didn't intend to startle your servant—it was I who was startled," replied Lady Death. "I was surprised to see your servant in Baghdad this morning, because I have an appointment with him in Sumera tonight."

You and I have an appointment. Perhaps it will be in London, Taipei, or Chicago. Wherever, it is one appointment we will not miss. As C. S. Lewis observed, the statistics on death are impressive—so far, it is one out of one!

Of course believers can be confident that we die in God's time. When Christ was told that His friend Lazarus was sick, He stayed away two extra days so that Lazarus would already be dead and buried by the time He arrived in Bethany. The sisters individually voiced their complaint, "If only You had been here, my brother would not have died." Yet Christ wanted them to understand that Lazarus had died within the will of God; he died according to the divine schedule.

In recent days I have conducted two funerals. The first was that of a Christian woman who had distinguished herself by a life of sacrificial service for Christ. The triumph of the family was striking; there was irrepressible joy mixed with the sorrow.

The second was that of an apparent unbeliever who was killed in a highway accident. The grief of the relatives was marked by desperation and hopelessness. They refused to be comforted.

We all are following those two people to the grave. Unless Christ should return in our lifetime, we will all pass through that iron gate described by Hamlet as "the undiscover'd country from whose bourn no traveler returns" (III, i, 80-81). The question is: Where will we be five minutes after we die?

I'm told that there is a cemetery in Indiana that has an old tombstone bearing this epitaph:

> Pause, Stranger, when you pass
>   me by
> As you are now, so once was I
> As I am now, so you will be
> So prepare for death and follow
>   me

An unknown passerby read those words and underneath scratched this reply:

> To follow you I'm not content
> Until I know which way you
>   went

The way we go is determined in this life. At death our destiny is unalterably fixed. For those who have admitted their sinfulness and received the free gift of eternal life through Jesus Christ, death leads to the realm called heaven, the abode of God.

Why is the contemplation of heaven so important for each of us? First, because it gives us perspective. Visualize a measuring tape extending from the earth to the farthest star. Our stay here would just be a hairline; it would be almost invisible compared to the length of the tape. Eternity is even longer, of course, and when that becomes our measuring rod the longest life is but a dot of time. That's why Paul says that the suffering of this present life cannot be compared with the glory that shall be revealed in us. Eternity gives perspective to time.

Second, the contemplation of heaven is crucial because we must use our time and resources to lay up treasures in heaven where moth and rust do not corrupt and where thieves do not break through and steal. Every one of us wants to make wise investments, to get the "biggest bang for our buck," as the saying goes. The best investments are those that are safe and permanent. Although entrance into heaven is a free gift, the extent of our inheritance will be determined by our faithfulness here on earth.

Imagine spending time redecorating a room of a house that is on fire! Why waste effort on that which is so temporary? Yet all that we have will be destroyed. Nothing we can see is forever. Why not send on ahead investments that will have permanent value and reward?

Recently I was browsing in the Travel section of a bookstore. Potential travelers choose from a dozen different books on Hawaii or Europe. They will be saving their money and making other sacrifices to prepare for their vacation, and though it will last but a few weeks they learn as much as they can about their destination. Some even try to learn the language of the country they intend to visit.

With heaven as our final destination, we should be learning all we can about that eternal home. The daughter of a fine Christian man who eventually died of cancer was heard to remark, "In Dad's final weeks he spent more time in heaven than he did on earth." And why not? The sufferings of this life often make us anxious to get on with the life to come. The certainty of heaven helps us cope with the uncertainties of earth.

A knowledge of heaven takes the sting out of death. A dying woman told her children, "Don't give me any further treatment. . . . Don't interfere with God's plan for my glorification." That represents the strong faith of one who walked with God for many years. There is no reason we cannot face death with the same degree of confidence. The apostle Paul looked forward to death, saying that he was ready to be offered, for the time of his departure had come.

Those of us who have close relatives who have died find another reason to learn what heaven will be like. We wonder what our friends are now doing; we try to visualize what it will be like to meet them someday. Paul taught that we have every right to know what God has revealed about the afterlife so that we will not grieve as those who have no hope. All believers will meet again. That gives comfort to the sorrowing.

How certain is heaven for the Christian? When Paul wanted to list all of the aspects of our salvation he wrote, "For whom He foreknew, he also predestined to become conformed to the image of His Son, that He might be the first-born among many brethren; and whom He predestined, these He also called; and whom He called, these He also justified; and whom He justified, these He also glorified" (Romans 8:29-30).

Notice that we are *already* glorified. In effect, our arrival in heaven has taken place. Those whom God chooses to be His—that is, those whom He foreknows and predestinates—are guaranteed a safe passage into their heavenly home. None is lost en route; in God's mind they have already arrived with their new bodies. For God "calls into being that which does not exist" (Romans 4:17).

In order to understand heaven, let us consider five new relationships that we will experience in the life to come.

A NEW BODY

We are a spiritual and physical unity. Our destiny includes the entirety of our being—body, soul, and spirit. In heaven we shall be the same people we are here on earth—the same body, soul, and spirit, though those three aspects will be adapted for heavenly existence. On the mount of transfiguration the disciples conversed with Moses and Elijah—the real Moses and Elijah. No replicas, no stand-ins.

THE CONTINUITY OF THE BODY

Some Christians assume that God will create new bodies for us out of nothing. But if that were so, there would be no need for the doctrine of resurrection. Paul's point in 1 Corinthians 15 is that our present physical bodies will be raised. "It is sown a perishable body, it is raised an imperishable body; it is sown in dishonor, it is raised in glory; it is sown in weakness, it is raised in power; it is sown a natural body, it is raised a spiritual body" (1 Corinthians 15:42-44). There is continuity between our earthly and our heavenly bodies.

Our future body will be like Christ's resurrection body. "We know that, when He appears, we shall be like Him, because we shall see Him just as He is" (1 John 3:2). Just think of the implications.

The continuity between Christ's earthly and heavenly body was clear to see—for example, the nail prints were in His hands. The disciples recognized Him instantly, and He even ate fish with them at the seashore. But there were also radical changes. He was able to travel from one place to another without physical effort and went through doors without opening them.

Evidently we too shall be able to travel effortlessly. Just as Christ could be in Galilee and then suddenly appear in Judea, so we shall be free from the limitations of terrestrial travel. That does not mean, of course, that we will be omnipresent as God is; we will be limited to one place at one time. But travel will be swift and effortless.

We can also expect that we shall have increased mental powers. "For now we see in a mirror dimly, but then face to face; now I know in part, but then I shall know fully just as I also have been fully known" (1 Corinthians 13:12). Again, we must remind ourselves that we shall not be omniscient, for the knowledge of all things is the special prerogative of God. But our minds will have keen perception without the limitations of a failing memory or fragmented comprehension. Like Adam before the Fall, our mental ability will operate at a high level.

There is good reason to expect that we shall continue learning in heaven. Our appreciation of God and His grace will grow throughout the ages. The famous Puritan writer Jonathan Edwards believed that the saints in heaven would begin by contemplating God's providential care of the church on earth and then move on to other aspects of the divine plan and thus "the ideas of the saints shall increase to eternity."

THE INTERMEDIATE STATE

Several views have arisen in the history of the church regarding the present status of the saints in heaven since they do not as yet have their permanent bodies. In about the seventh century the Roman Catholic church began teaching the doctrine of purgatory, not because it was found in the Bible but because of the church's view of justification. The teaching was that no one dies completely righteous in God's sight; therefore souls need to be purged by fire before entering heaven. The length of stay depends on the amount of time needed to finish the process of salvation.

Martin Luther, while studying the book of Romans, came to understand that justification means that God declares us to be as righteous as Christ despite our present imperfections. Thus souls go directly to heaven, accepted by God on the basis of the complete merit of Christ. That teaching put the doctrine of salvation on a firm footing and also explains why the thief on the cross was assured fellowship with Christ in paradise on that very day. The doctrine of purgatory must be rejected.

Others, such as Seventh Day Adventists, teach that the soul sleeps until the resurrection of the body. Those who die in the Lord are at this moment unconscious. They shall be awakened when the Lord shall come with the sound of a trumpet and the dead in Christ are raised.

The teaching of soul sleep is based on those passages where the word *sleep* is used to refer to those who have died (John 11:11; Acts 7:60; 1 Corinthians 15:51). However, we must realize that in each instance those Scriptures refer to the sleep of the body, not the sleep of the soul. The body sleeps until the resurrection, but the soul is conscious. That is proved by many Scriptures teaching that believers are immediately taken to heaven at death and are conscious in His presence (Luke 23:43; Philippians 1:23).

That leads us to a question that has puzzled theologians: Since the resurrection of the body is future, are the present saints in heaven disembodied spirits? Or do they have some kind of a temporary "intermediate" body that will be discarded on the day of resurrection—the day when we all receive our permanent, glorified bodies?

The point of disagreement is over Paul's words in 2 Corinthians 5:1, "For we know that if the earthly tent which is our house is torn down, we have a building from God, a house not made with hands, eternal in the heavens." The question is: To what period in the future does he refer when he speaks of our having "a building of God . . . eternal in the heavens"? Do we have that building at death, or do we receive it at the future resurrection? Paul shrinks from the idea that his soul would live through a period of nakedness, a time when it would exist without a body.

Some scholars teach that the saints who have died already now have bodies, temporary bodies that will be replaced by their eternal bodies at the time of resurrection. This view is attractive because it explains how the redeemed in heaven can relate to Christ and to one another. If departed believers can sing the praises of God and communicate to one another, it seems that they must have a body in which to do so. What is more, at the point of transition between life and death some have actually testified that they have already seen departed relatives awaiting their arrival. That points to the conclusion that the saints in heaven already have recognizable bodies.

On the mount of transfiguration, Moses and Elijah appeared in some kind of body. Admittedly, Elijah was taken up to heaven and therefore may not have needed to await the resurrection—he may have his permanent body already. But Moses was buried on Mount Nebo and was awaiting a future resurrection. Though he has as yet not received that eternal resurrection body, he already appeared with Christ two thousand years ago, recognizable to the disciples and communicating with them. The rich man who died and went to Hades evidently had a body, since he was able to use human speech and wanted his tongue cooled with water.

However, we must ask ourselves, if the saints already have bodies in heaven (albeit temporary ones), why does Paul place such an emphasis on the resurrection in his writings? He does imply that the saints in heaven today are incomplete; they are in an unnatural state.

So a second plausible explanation might be that the souls of the departed dead may in some ways have the functions of a body. If that is the case, it would explain how they can communicate with one another and have a visible presence in heaven. These capabilities of the soul are implied in Revelation 6:9-10. "And when He broke the fifth seal, I saw underneath the altar the *souls* of those who had been slain because of the word of God, and because of the testimony which they had maintained; and they cried out with a loud voice, saying, 'How long, O Lord, holy and true, wilt Thou refrain from judging and avenging our blood on those who dwell on the earth?' " (italics mine). We then read that they were even given white robes to wear as they waited for God to avenge them.

Admittedly the word *psychas* (translated "souls") has a broad meaning and can also be translated "lives" or "persons." But the word is often translated *soul* as distinguished from the body. If that is what John meant, it would give credence to the view that souls can take upon themselves shape and bodily characteristics. If that seems strange to us, it may well be that our concept of the soul is too limited.

We cannot be sure about which of those views is correct. Of this much we may be certain: believers go directly into the presence of Christ at death. They are conscious and in command of all of their faculties. As D. L. Moody said before he died, "Soon you will read in the papers that Moody is dead . . . don't believe it . . . for in that moment I will be more alive than I have ever been."

THE AGE OF THE BODY

What about infants who have died? Since there is continuity between the earthly and heavenly body, will they be infants forever?

Parents who have lost a child rightly wonder whether their child has made a safe arrival in heaven. The answer, I believe, is yes, though we must be clear as to why we believe they will be saved. Contrary to popular opinion, children will not be in heaven because they are innocent. Paul taught clearly that children are born under the condemnation of Adam's sin (Romans 5:12). Indeed, it is because they are born sinners that they experience death.

Nor should we make a distinction between children who are baptized and those who are not, as if such a ritual can make one a child of God. The idea of infant baptism arose in North Africa years after the New Testament was written. Even if it can be justified theologically as a sign of the covenant (a debatable proposition), there is no evidence whatever that it can give to children the gift of eternal life.

If children are saved (and I believe they shall be) it can only be because God credits their sin to Christ; and because they are too young to believe, the requirement of personal faith is waived. We do not know at what age they are held personally accountable. It is impossible to suggest an age, since that may vary, depending on the child's capacity and mental development.

Though the Bible is not clear on the subject, there are strong indications that children who die are with the Lord. David lost two sons for whom he grieved deeply. For Absalom, his rebellious son, he wept uncontrollably and refused comfort, for he was uncertain about the young man's destiny. But when the child born to Bathsheba died, he washed, anointed himself, and came into the house of the Lord to worship. He gave this explanation to those who asked about his behavior: "Now he has died; why should I fast? Can I bring him back again? I shall go to him, but he will not return to me" (2 Samuel 12:23).

Christ saw children as being in close proximity to God and the kingdom of heaven. "See that you do not despise one of these little ones, for I say to you, that their angels in heaven continually behold the face of My Father who is in heaven" (Matthew 18:10). Children are close to the heart of God.

Will a baby always be a baby in heaven? James Vernon McGee has made the interesting suggestion that God will resurrect the infants as they are and that the mothers' arms that have ached for them will have the opportunity of holding their little ones. The father who never had the opportunity of holding that little hand will be given that privilege. Thus the children will grow up with their parents.

Whether that will be the case, we do not know. But of this we can be confident: a child in heaven will be complete. Either the child will look as he would have if he were full grown, or else his mental and physical capacities will be enhanced to give him full status among the redeemed. Heaven is not a place for second-class citizens; all handicaps are removed. Heaven is a place of perfection.

The death of an infant, however, causes all of us to struggle with the will and purpose of God. It seems strange that God would grant the gift of life and then cause it to be snuffed out before it could blossom into a stage of usefulness. But we can be sure that there is a purpose in such a life, even if it is not immediately discernable.

James Vernon McGee again says that when a shepherd seeks to lead his sheep to better grass up the winding, thorny mountain paths, he often finds that the sheep will not follow him. They fear the unknown ridges and the sharp rocks. The shepherd will then reach into the flock and take a little lamb in one arm and another on his other arm. Then he starts up the precipitous pathway. Soon the two mother sheep begin to follow and afterward the entire flock. Thus they ascend the torturous path to greener pastures.

So it is with the Good Shepherd. Sometimes He reaches into the flock and takes a lamb to Himself. He uses the experience to lead His people, to lift them to new heights of commitment as they follow the little lamb all the way home.

A little girl died in a hotel where she was staying with her father. Since her mother was already dead, just two followed the body to the cemetery—the father and the minister. The man grieved uncontrollably as he took the key and unlocked the casket to look upon the face of his child one last time. Then he closed the casket and handed the key to the keeper of the cemetery. On the way back the minister quoted Revelation 1:17*b*-18 to the broken-hearted man. "'Do not be afraid; I am the first and the last, and the living One; and I was dead, and behold, I am alive forevermore, and I have the keys of death and of Hades.'

"You think the key to your little daughter's casket is in the hands of the keeper of the cemetery," the minister said. "But the key is in the hands of the Son of God, and He will come some morning and use it."

The words comforted the heart of the grieving father for he understood the meaning of the resurrection.

In heaven we shall experience our new resurrection bodies, perfect in beauty and power. We shall be able to use our bodies and minds to serve the Savior and to express to Him our eternal adoration. Let me quote once more John's incredible words: "We know that, when He appears, we shall be like Him, because we shall see Him just as He is" (1 John 3:2b).

A NEW HOME

Though a glorified body can live quite comfortably in this world (as Christ did after the resurrection) God has prepared a new home for the redeemed of all ages. Christ assured the disciples that the place He was preparing had "many dwelling places." There would be plenty of room for all of the redeemed.

John gives us this description: "And I saw a new heaven and a new earth; for the first heaven and the first earth passed away, and there is no longer any sea. And I saw the holy city, new Jerusalem, coming down out of heaven from God, made ready as a bride adorned for her husband" (Revelation 21:1-2).

This city is new—that is, re-created—just as our resurrected bodies are re-created from our earthly bodies. The previous heavens (the atmospheric heavens) and the earth, tainted by sin, will have been dissolved by fire to make room for the new order of creation (2 Peter 3:7-13).

This city came out of heaven. It originates from heaven because it is part of the heavenly realm. This is the most detailed description of what heaven will be like. Let's consider some features of this beautiful permanent home.

The dimensions are given as a cube, 1,500 miles square. "And the city is laid out as a square, and its length is as great as the width; and he measured the city with the rod, fifteen hundred miles; its length and width and height are equal" (Revelation 21:16).

If we take that literally, heaven will be composed of 396,000 stories (at twenty feet per story) each having an area as big as one half the size of the United States! Divide that up into separate condominiums, and you have plenty of room for all who have been redeemed by God since the beginning of time. The Old Testament saints, Abraham, Isaac, and Jacob—they will be there. Then we think of the New Testament apostles and all the redeemed throughout two thousand years of church history— heaven will be the home for all of them. Unfortunately, however, the majority of the world's population will likely not be there. Heaven, as Christ explained, is a special place for special people.

You need not fear that you will be lost in the crowd; nor need you fear being stuck on the thousandth floor when all of the activity is in the downstairs lounge. All that you will need to do is to decide where you would like to be, and you will be there! Each occupant will receive individualized attention. The Good Shepherd who calls His own sheep by name will have a special place prepared for each of His lambs. As someone has said, there will be a crown awaiting us that no one else can wear, a dwelling place that no one else can enter.

THE MATERIALS OF THE CITY

The details can be written, though hardly imagined. In John Bunyan's *Pilgrim's Progress*, as Christian and Hopeful finally see the City of God, there was such beauty that they fell sick with happiness, crying out, "If you see my Beloved, tell Him I am sick with love." The city was so glorious that they could not yet look upon it directly but had to use an instrument made for that purpose. This, after all, is the dwelling place of God.

John wrote in Revelation that the city had the glory of God. "Her brilliance was like a very costly stone, as a stone of crystal-clear jasper" (21:11). It is interesting that the city shares some features of the earthly Jerusalem, but we are more impressed with the contrasts. The new Jerusalem is a city of unimaginable beauty and brilliance.

First, there is a wall with twelve foundation stones that encompasses the city. "And the wall of the city had twelve foundation stones, and on them were the twelve names of the twelve apostles of the Lamb" (21:14).

As for the foundation stones on which the wall is built, each is adorned with a different kind of precious stone—the list is in 21:19-20. The jewels roughly parallel the twelve stones in the breastplate of the high priest (Exodus 28:17-20).

The height of the wall is given as seventy-two yards, not very high in comparison to the massive size of the city. But high enough to provide security and to make sure that it is accessible only through proper entrances.

Second, we notice the twelve gates, each a single pearl (Revelation 21:12, 21). That is a reminder that entrance to the city is restricted; only those who belong are admitted "and nothing unclean and no one who practices abomination and lying, shall ever come into it, but only those whose names are written in the Lamb's book of life" (v. 27).

John gives a further description of those who are outside the city walls. "Outside are the dogs and the sorcerers and the immoral persons and the murderers and the idolaters, and everyone who loves and practices lying" (22:15). There is a sentinel angel at each gate, evidently to make sure that only those who have their names written in the book are admitted.

The twelve gates are divided into four groups, thus three gates face each of the four directions. "There were three gates on the east and three gates on the north and three gates on the south and three gates on the west"(21:13). That is a reminder that the gospel is for all men, and all the tribes of the earth will be represented.

Notice that the saints of the Old Testament and the New are both included. The names of the twelve sons of Israel are written on the gates of the city, and the New Testament apostles have their names inscribed on the foundation stones. Thus the unity of the people of God throughout all ages is evident.

As for the street of the city it was "pure gold, like transparent glass" (v. 21). It is illuminated by the glory of God, and the Lamb is the lamp.

Now we can better understand why Bunyan said that the pilgrims must see the city through a special instrument. Its beauty is simply too much for us to comprehend. We need a transformed body and mind to behold it with unrestricted admiration.

When Christ said He was preparing a home for us with many mansions, He did not imply, as some have suggested, that He needed plenty of time to do the building. God is able to create the heavenly Jerusalem in a moment of time. But Christ did emphasize that we would be with Him, and we know that His presence will even be more marvelous than our environment.

A New Occupation

It's been estimated that there are at least 40,000 different occupations in the United States. Yet, for all that, only a small percentage of the population is completely satisfied with their responsibilities. Personnel problems, the lack of adequate pay, and wearisome hours of routine tasks are only some of the reasons. Few, if any, are truly satisfied.

But those problems will be behind us forever in heaven. Each job description will entail two primary responsibilities. First, there will be the worship of God; second, there will be the serving of the Most High in whatever capacity that is assigned to us.

Let's try to capture the privilege of worship.

Heaven is first and foremost the dwelling place of God. It is true, of course, that God's presence is not limited to heaven, for He is omnipresent. Solomon perceptively commented, "Behold, heaven and the highest heaven cannot contain Thee, how much less this house which I have built!" (1 Kings 8:27).

Yet in heaven God is localized. John saw God seated upon a throne with twenty-four other thrones occupied by twenty-four elders who worship the King. "And from the throne proceed flashes of lightning and sounds and peals of thunder" (Revelation 4:5). And what is the nature of the activity around that throne? There is uninhibited joy and spontaneous worship.

Needless to say the saints on earth are imperfect. They are beset by quarrels, carnality, and doctrinal deviations. Read a book on church history and you will marvel that the church has survived these two thousand years.

Have you ever wondered what it would be like to belong to a perfect church? That is precisely what John saw when he peered into heaven.

Free from the limitations of the flesh and the opposition of the devil, the perfect church is found singing the praises of Christ without self-consciousness or mixed motives.

Repeatedly John sees worship taking place in heaven. Even after the judgment of God is heaped upon unrepentant sinners, the saints join with other created beings to chant the praises of God:

> And a voice came from the throne, saying, "Give praise to our God, all you His bond-servants, you who fear Him, the small and the great." And I heard, as it were, the voice of a great multitude and as the sound of many waters and as the sound of mighty peals of thunder, saying, "Hallelujah! For the Lord our God, the Almighty, reigns" (Revelation 19:5-6).

If we want to prepare for our final destination, we should begin to worship God here on earth. Our arrival in heaven will only be a continuation of what we have already begun. Praise is the language of heaven and the language of the faithful on earth.

SERVICE TO THE LORD

Though worship shall occupy much of our time in heaven, we will also be assigned responsibilities commensurate with the faithfulness we displayed here on earth: "And His bond-servants shall serve Him; and they shall see His face, and His name shall be on their foreheads" (Revelation 22:3*b*-4).

That word *servant* is found frequently in the book of Revelation for it pictures a continuation of the relationship we even now have with Christ. However, the word *serve* used here is used primarily in the New Testament for service that is carried on within the Temple or church (Matthew 4:10; Luke 2:37; Acts 24:14). Thus we shall serve Him in that special, intimate relationship available only to those who are included within the inner circle of the redeemed. David Gregg gives his conception of what that kind of work will be like:

> It is work as free from care and toil and fatigue as is the wing-stroke of the jubilant lark when it soars into the sunlight of a fresh, clear day and, spontaneously and for self-relief, pours out its thrilling carol. Work up there is a matter of self-relief, as well as a matter of obedience to the ruling will of God. It is work according to one's tastes and delight and ability. If tastes vary there, if abilities vary there, then occupations will vary there.[1]

What responsibilities will we have? Christ told a parable that taught that the faithful were given authority over cities. Most scholars believe that will be fulfilled during the millennial kingdom when we shall rule with Christ here on earth. But it is reasonable to assume that there is continuity between the earthly kingdom and the eternal heavenly kingdom. In other words it may well be that our faithfulness (or unfaithfulness) on earth may have repercussions throughout eternity.

Yes, everyone in heaven will be happy and fulfilled. Everyone will be assigned a place in the administration of the vast heavenly kingdom. But just as there are varied responsibilities in the palace of an earthly king, so in heaven some will be given more prominent responsibilities than others.

Of this we may be certain: heaven is not a place of inactivity or boredom. It is not, as a Sunday school pupil thought, an interminable worship service where we begin on page one of the hymnal and sing all the way through. God will have productive work for us to do. We will increase our knowledge of Him and His wondrous works. Will not Christ show us the Father that we might be forever satisfied? Will we not then learn to love the Lord our God in ways that we have never been able to do on earth?

We do not know, as some have speculated, whether we shall explore other worlds. Others have suggested that we shall be able to complete many projects begun on earth. Whatever our activity, we can be sure that our infinite heavenly Father will have infinite possibilities.

A NEW FAMILY

We were created for the pleasure of God. His purpose was that at least some human beings would be in fellowship with Him forever.

In Eden, Adam walked with God in the cool of the day.

After the Tabernacle was built, the Shekinah glory settled in the Holy of Holies and among the people to give visible evidence that God was dwelling among them.

In this church age, the presence of God has been transferred to believers as they meet together in the name of Christ. Even more specifically, our bodies are the "temple of the Holy Spirit."

In heaven all of those relationships will be changed so that we will be in the presence of Christ without the limitations of sin. The barriers that hide the face of God will be lifted, and we shall "see Him as he is."

We often wonder whether the family relationships of earth will still be in existence in heaven. The Sadducees, who did not believe in the resurrection of the body, came to Christ with this puzzle: If a man is married on earth and his wife dies and he chooses to remarry, and the pattern repeats itself seven times—who will his wife be at the resurrection? Christ chided them, saying they knew neither the Scriptures nor the power of God. In heaven the marriage relationship does not exist.

That does not mean that in heaven we will be sexless (i.e., neither male nor female). Your mother will still be known as your mother in heaven; your father will be known as he was here on earth. Christ is simply saying that in heaven there is no marriage—there will be no babies born. Just as the angels are not reproduced by procreation, so the sexual relationship will no longer be a part of the divine order.

Will we still have a special relationship with family members? Think of it this way: The intimacy you now enjoy with your family will be expanded to include all the other saints that are present. Even in the Old Testament there was a recognition that saints would know one another in the life beyond. When a man died it was said, "He was gathered to his people."

One day some of Christ's friends sent word that His mother and brothers were looking for Him. Christ responded, "Who are My mother and My brothers?" And looking around Him, He said, "Behold, My mother and My brothers! For whoever does the will of God, he is My brother and sister and mother" (Mark 3:33-35).

Think of the implications: we will be just as close to Christ as we are to any member of our present family. Indeed, He is not ashamed to call us His brothers! There will be extended family with greater intimacy than we have known on earth.

Archbishop Whately has an excellent description of the kind of friendship we can expect in heaven:

> I am convinced that the extension and perfection of friendship will constitute a great part of the future happiness of the blest. . . . A wish to see and personally know, for example, the apostle Paul, or John, is the most likely to arise in the noblest and purest mind. I should be sorry to think such a wish absurd and presumptuous, or unlikely ever to be gratified. The highest enjoyment doubtless to the blest will be the personal knowledge of their great and beloved Master. Yet I cannot but think that some part of their happiness will con-

sist in an intimate knowledge of the greatest of His followers also; and of those of them in particular, whose peculiar qualities are, to each, the most peculiarly attractive.[2]

Think of the joys of such a family! And of the infinite time to become better acquainted.

A New Order of Reality

Fortunately heaven will not have everything. In fact, John lists many different experiences and realities known on earth that will be absent there.

No more sea. Throughout the Bible the word *sea* stands for the nations of the world, usually the rebellious nations. Heaven means that the strife between nations and the seething turmoil that accompanies those struggles will vanish. No broken treaties, no wars, no scandals.

No more death. The hearse will have made its last journey. Today we look at death as a thief that robs us of our earthly existence. It is simply the final act in the deterioration of the human body. As such it is almost universally feared; no one can escape its terrors. Even Christians who have conquered it in Christ may tremble at its fearsome onslaught. But death shall not enter heaven. No funeral services, no tombstones, no tearful good-byes.

No more sorrow. Read the newspaper, and sorrow is written on every page. An automobile accident takes the life of a young father; a child is raped by a madman; a flood in Bangladesh kills 20,000. No one can fathom the amount of emotional pain borne by the inhabitants of this world in any single moment. In heaven there will be uninterrupted joy and emotional tranquillity.

No more crying. No one could possibly calculate the buckets of tears that are shed every single moment in this hurting world. From the child crying because of the death of a parent to the woman weeping because of a failed marriage—multiply those tears by a million, and you will realize that we live in a crying world.

In heaven, He who wiped away our sins now wipes away our tears. This comment has raised the question of why there would be tears in heaven in the first place. And does the Lord come with a handkerchief and literally wipe away each tear? That is possible. But I think that John means more than that. He wants us to understand that God will give us an explanation for the sorrow we experienced on earth so that we will not have to cry anymore. If that were not so, then the tears might return after He has wiped them away. But being able to view the tearful events of earth from the perspective of heaven will dry up our tears forever.

The question is often asked how we can be happy in heaven if one or more of our relatives is in hell. Can a child, for example, enjoy the glories of eternity knowing that a father or a mother will always be absent from the celebration? Or can a godly mother serve and worship with joy knowing that her precious son will be in torment forever? That question has so vexed the minds of theologians that some have actually asserted that in heaven God will blank out a part of our memory. The child will not know that his parents are lost in hell; the mother will not remember that she had a son.

However, it is unlikely that we will know less in heaven than we do on earth. It is not characteristic of God to resolve a problem by expanding the sphere of human ignorance. That is especially true in heaven, where we will have better mental faculties than on earth. In heaven we shall be comforted, not because we know less than we did on earth but because we know more.

It is more likely that God will wipe away all tears by explaining His ultimate purposes. We will look at heaven and hell from His viewpoint and say that He did all things well. If God can be content knowing that unbelievers are in hell, so will we.

I expect that all who are in heaven will live with the knowledge that justice was fully served and that God's plan was right. And with such an explanation and perspective, our emotions will mirror those of our heavenly Father. Jonathan Edwards said that heaven will have no pity for hell, not because the saints are unloving but because they are perfectly loving. They will see everything in conformity with God's love, justice, and glory. Thus with both head and heart we will worship the Lord without regret, sorrow, or misgivings about our Father's plan.

No more pain. Come with me as we walk down the corridor of a hospital. Here is a young mother dying of cancer; a man is gasping for breath, trying to overcome the terror of a heart attack. In the next ward an abused child has just been admitted with burns inflicted by an angry father. For those and countless other emergencies scientists have prepared painkillers to help people make it through life, one day at a time.

In heaven pain, which is the result of sin, is banished forever. No headaches, slipped discs, or surgery. And no more emotional pain because of rejection, separation, or abuse.

No Temple. Some have been puzzled by that assertion because elsewhere John says that there is a Temple in heaven (Revelation 11:19). Wilbur M. Smith points out that the apparent contradiction can be resolved when we realize that the Temple and its angelic messengers "continue in action during the time of man's sin and the outpouring of the wrath of God, but after the old earth has disappeared, the temple has no longer any function."[3] The worship in heaven is now carried on directly; God Himself is the shrine, the Temple. The former patterns of worship give way to a new, unrestricted order.

No more sun or moon. Those planets created by God to give light to the earth have outlived their purpose. God Himself is the light of heaven. "And the city has no need of the sun or of the moon to shine upon it, for the glory of God has illumined it, and its lamp is the Lamb" (Revelation 21:23). Again we read, "And there shall no longer be any night; and they shall not have need of the light of a lamp nor the light of the sun, because the Lord God shall illumine them; and they shall reign forever and ever" (22:5).

That means that the holy city is interpenetrated with light. Joseph Seiss explains it this way:

> That shining is not from any material combustion, not from any consumption of fuel that needs to be replaced as one supply burns out; for it is the uncreated light of Him who is light, dispensed by and through the Lamb as the everlasting Lamp, to the home, and hearts, and understandings of His glorified saints.[4]

No abominations. The nations shall bring the honor and glory of God into the city, but we read, "Nothing unclean and no one who practices abomination and lying shall ever come into it, but only those whose names are written in the Lamb's book of life" (21:27). John lists others who will be excluded: immoral people, murderers, idolaters, and the like.

No more hunger, thirst, or heat. Those burdens borne by the multitudes of this present world will vanish forever. In their place will be the tree of life and the beauty of the paradise of God.

Those things that cast such a pall of gloom over the earth today will be replaced by indescribable happiness in the presence of Divine Glory.

Just think of stepping on shore
And finding it heaven
Of clasping a hand
And finding it God's
Of breathing new air
And finding it celestial
Of waking up in glory
And finding it home.[5]

CHECKING YOUR PASSPORT

Those of us who have traveled in foreign countries know the importance of a passport. Regardless of your status and charisma, that document is what qualifies you for entry and acceptance among the people in a different land.

There is nothing quite like coming home to the land of your own citizenship. If you are an American there is no fear in returning to America—you know that your entry is assured.

We have a passport to get into heaven, the country where we claim citizenship. In fact we have already established residence there, for all believers are "seated with Christ in the heavenlies." That means we will not have a hassle at the border but are guaranteed entry. Only those who are prepared to die are prepared to live.

What is Christ's attitude toward our homecoming? Repeatedly in the New Testament Christ is spoken of as sitting "at the right hand of God." But there is one reference to Christ's leaving His seat and standing; He is welcoming one of His servants home. As Stephen was being stoned, we read that "being full of the Holy Spirit, he gazed intently into heaven and saw the glory of God, and Jesus standing at the right hand of God" (Acts 7:55).

Thus the seated Son of God stood to welcome one of His own into the heavenly realm. A believer's death may be unnoticed on earth, but is front page news in heaven. The Son of God takes note.

No one can enter heaven without God's specific approval. Each one must have a passport signed by His own Son. Those who receive it may enter those gates; all others must stay outside. Those who have the passport need not fear saying good-bye to earth, for they are assured a welcome in heaven. A little girl was asked whether she feared walking through the cemetery. She replied, "No, because my home is on the other side."

D. L. Moody at death caught a glimpse of heaven. Awakening from sleep he said, "Earth recedes, Heaven opens before me. If this is death, it is sweet! There is no valley here. God is calling me and I must go!"

43

Remember the words of Hamlet in Shakespeare's play? In a moment of deep contemplation he mused, "To be, or not to be, that is the question" (III, i, 57). He was contemplating suicide because life had become unbearable. Yet when he thought of where that might lead him, he continued, "In that sleep of death what dreams may come when we have shuffled off this mortal coil" (III, i, 67-68). He wondered whether his existence on the other side might be even more intolerable than life.

Compare that with the words of Paul, "But I am hard-pressed from both directions, having the desire to depart and be with Christ, for that is very much better; yet to remain on in the flesh is more necessary for your sake" (Philippians 1:23-24).

Hamlet says, "Live or die, I lose!" Paul says, "Live or die, I win!"

Knowing Christ makes the difference.

Notes

1. David Gregg, *The Heaven-Life* (New York: Revell, 1895), p. 62.
2. Richard Whately, *A View of the Scripture Revelations Concerning a Future State* (3d ed., Philadelphia: Lindsay & Blakiston, 1857), pp. 214-15.
3. Wilbur M. Smith, *Biblical Doctrine of Heaven* (Chicago: Moody, 1968), p. 253.
4. Joseph Seiss, *Lectures on the Apocalypse* (New York: Charles C. Cook, 1901), III:412-13. Quoted in Wilbur Smith, p. 249.
5. "Finally Home," reprinted with permission of Benson Company, Inc. Copyright 1971 by Singspiration Music.